MW01164706

Merrimac Mic Takes the Fifth:
Anthology V

Also from Merrimac Mic

Merrimac Mic Anthology:
gleanings from the first year

Merrimac Mic Anthology II:
going with the floes

Merrimac Mic Anthology III:
the river widens

Merrimac Mic Anthology IV:
watershed

Merrimac Mic Takes the Fifth: Anthology V

Edited by Isabell VanMerlin

Cover and book design
Isabell VanMerlin

Cover photo
October sunset on the Merrimack River
Paulette Demers Turco

The authors may be contacted via their e-mail addresses, which are stated under their names.

Merrimac Mic Takes the Fifth: Anthology V is a compilation of poetry and other writings.

ISBN: 9781795002776

This book is available from
Amazon.com
and by order from most booksellers.

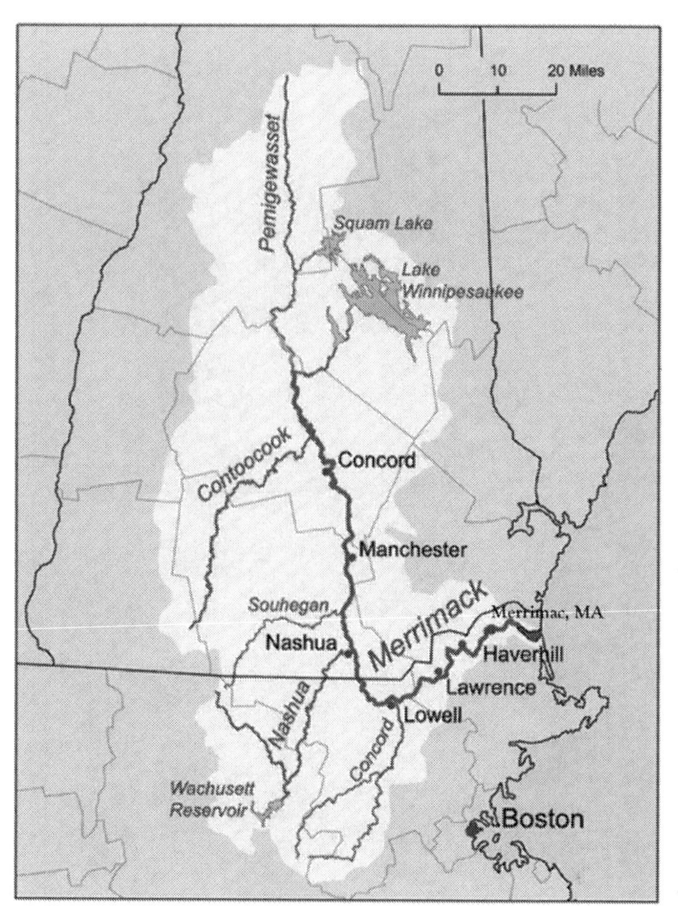

The Merrimack River

Cover photo info:

October Sunset on the Merrimack River was taken by Paulette Demers Turco beside the Rocks Village Drawbridge which connects West Newbury to Haverhill and Merrimac, MA. The view is southwest from West Newbury's shore. Although the river originates in Franklin in the White Mountains of New Hampshire, it travels south as far as Lowell, MA, then curves northeast to empty into the Atlantic between Salisbury and Plum Island, Newburyport, MA.

This map shows the watershed area of the Merrimack in recent years. Before the last glacial period, the Merrimack emptied into the Atlantic further south around Boston.

If you think anyone has come to Merrimac Mic and taken the Fifth, they will not be in this anthology! The whole point of an open mic is to spill your words, songs or guts to a sympathetic audience. It doesn't have to be the truth, though!

Contents

Introduction

[Editor's note: What better way to introduce a poetry anthology than with a totally appropriate poem about the river from which we take our name? And a beautiful poem it is.]

Almost Whole

The sea runs tonight.
The moon is almost full.
Stand with me at the narrow straits,
where the Merrimack meets the tide.
Gaze across the bay, under the gibbous night,
watch at anchor, how the island rides.
Against the dark, it plumbs the deepening sea.
Breathe in the cool night-air, and look!
Even the wind on the water moves to the lunar pull!
Keeping her date, the moon rests on our shoulders.
Starlight gleams from a distant shore.
Moon-blanched rocks stand above the flood,
the Joppa Flats are gone. Salt-marsh birds rest in the reeds.
Tonight they hide, choosing to let the tide work its force.
Keeping her promise, on her ephemeris, the moon moves,
the waters rise, and our river changes course,
bearing in the salt, a salve for the wounded.
Tonight we receive the tide's ephemeral and ageless balm.

In this long arrival of life, I am reached
by a tide that stands full at the strand.
The water lies full at my feet, cresting
where I stand, where I am, cresting the shore.
Good comes in, comes in, to me as to each,
retreats and then, calls out, have some more.
In this run, ebbs strife.
Good flows in, arriving, and arriving.
It is enough. I take, I sample, I store.

Tonight there is no retreat,
no gliding taking in the wash of the strand,
no draw of the tide, no grating roar.
Tonight the same salten sea rises within;
the same ocean river courses the inner shore.
It runs in this temple, in these freshets and veins.
Tonight it arrives, bearing the same cure.
I am not as wounded as I thought –
no knife to withdraw.
I am speechless, struck dumb to my shallow core
by the depth of the sea that surrounds.
The breath of the sea-air touches my face,
sea and stars go still; wind and water, no sound.
From afar, tide and moon in silent tune embrace.
I see no struggle, no pain, no sadness, no sorrow –
no need. The moon is almost full.

What if I am standing at the waters of Charon,
in range of his searching eye? The ferryman, ready on his raft,
ready with his constrictors, his leathers, his binds,
gliding by, on the dark river Styx, silent, his eye all hunger –
what if he found me with no want, no hunger, no need?
What if he turned downstream?
Tonight the ferryman turns his eye,
and misses one.
Ready with his constrictors, he turns from me,
and I unwind what was taut.
The cord of discord is loosed, prevented, undone.
I have finally gone to school. I have finally learned
how to be untaught.
What I have is enough.
The night-air is sweet. The tide is full.
The darkling plain but reveals
the glimmering light of the stars.

-Mark Bohrer

Postscript to *Almost Whole*

a poetic response to *Dover Beach*

One of my favorite poems is *Dover Beach* by Matthew Arnold. I hesitate to say this because it's such a downbeat poem. Oh my God, I swear, if Mr. Arnold had a pistol nearby when he completed it, it might have been all over. And yet, for us in America today, it's easier than ever to relate to Arnold's downbeat view of the human condition and human fate that's found in *Dover Beach.* "Darkling plain" indeed!

Matthew Arnold's poem is short, less than 40 lines, and very accessible. And yet it has so many layers and echoes for such a short poem. There's a good chance you read it in high school. It's been called "the most anthologized poem in the English language."

I've carried this poem around in my head for most of my life. The thing is, as beautiful as it is, and as evocative as it is, I couldn't disagree with it more. So in addition to the words of this poem, I carried THAT thought in my head for quite a while too. Somehow, Mr. Arnold got it fundamentally - if beautifully - wrong.

Well, as I carried these thoughts around, something happened, as things do. This mulling turned into a poem - one that actually started out in response to something else - but somehow in the end became a response to *Dover Beach.*

-Mark Bohrer

About the poet:
Engineering. Computers. Project management. And still room in the same brain for poetry and a connection to the life of the spirit. Why not? Mark Bohrer is currently the Poet Laureate of North Andover. You can find more of his poetry, thoughts and favorite poems at www.markbohrer.us.

Acknowledgments

It's Elizabeth's fault that Merrimac Mic is still extant. She refused to let it be shut down when Isabell moved from Newburyport too far west to be able to make it to the Thursday night meets – and Elizabeth didn't want to drive at night anyway – and so the new venue was found, by said Elizabeth, very convenient to her residence … allowing her to walk to Merrimac Mic.

And here she is, shouldering on! Thank you, Elizabeth!

And we have Jim Knowles to thank for the podium that Elizabeth is shouldering – plus the mic stand – and his assembling of our accoutrements every time we meet! Thank you, too, Jim!

Words can be heavy . . . *and* flammable. Lucky we have a Fire Lane.

This collection of words is acknowledgment in itself of the poets, storytellers, artists and their words and images. I, Isabell VanMerlin, however, would like to thank everyone for sharing their thoughts with me because I perceive them as personal gifts, given to *me*. I want you all to know how much pleasure it gives me to see and hear your words and know that you are being yourselves. I'm into Truth and Real and Fun. And you have shown up and expressed. Thank you!

AND
Merrimac Mic at Merrimac Library
our wonderful venue -
Thank you, thank you to you, too!!

detail from *October Sunset*
Paulette Demers Turco

Matinal

Sweet life on the waterfront,
summery town,
I fear your reflection
may shiver and drown.

Who is that figure
sat hunched on the pier,
cowering, rigid
with animal fear?

Foolish anxiety,
older and wiser?
Providence dressed in
the rags of a miser?

Life without struggle,
life without care,
why do you whisper
Beware, Beware?

-*Alfred Nicol*
alfred.nicol@comcast.net

About the poet:
Alfred Nicol's most recent collection of poetry, *Animal Psalms*, was published in 2016, by Able Muse Press. Two other collections: *Elegy for Everyone*, was published 2009, and *Winter Light*, received the 2004 Richard Wilbur Award. "Addendum" was included in *The Best American Poetry 2018.*

Wrestling the Devil

The minister's daughter steps inside
And latches shut the door,
As Patch, who has traipsed the fields with her
Flops down upon the floor.

The embers in the fireplace,
That keep the chill at bay,
Slow with their flickering, reddish light
The dwindling of the day.

She too lies down and rests her legs
On the couch, where she can see
The titles of the hundreds of books
In her father's library.

He's added to his stacks of books—
She finds, among several more,
A work by the scientist, Dawkins,
She'd never seen before.

She pulls it from the shelf and reads
These words that make no sense:
"Faith is belief in spite of—*because* of—
The lack of evidence."

She closes the book and shuts her eyes
And feels the darkness seep,
Drenching her chest, her legs and her arms
With the heaviness of sleep.

A shadow lunges toward her
And pins her where she lies.
She struggles, desperate to break free,
Bound with unbreakable ties.

She fights with all her mortal strength
Against the force astride her,
But cannot get ahold of this—
This darkness from inside her.

She knows him for a devil then
And calls him by that name.
The shadow backs away, but pulls
An iron from the flame.

He brands her where the sock fell down
To bare her pale white skin,
Still jeering as he slinks away,
"All right. For *now*, you win."

Then only faithful Patch remains,
Who's growling at the door,
Till he turns around to lie at her feet,
Licking the open sore.

~Alfred Nicol

Samuel Clemens

Samuel Clemens spent most of his life
  scheming to make a killing.
America gets its real work done
  in spite of itself, God willing.

A Confluence

For Thoreau's bicentennial, artist Diane Szczepaniak created a "River of Sticks" at Hopgood Wright Forest in Concord, MA.

Childlike, like hide-and-seek,
to gather broken limbs...
Through art, technique,

or magic out of Grimm's,
with them she'll build a stream
the strider skims

and, caught up in the dream,
she'll tuck a twig in where
the ripples seem

to leave their bed, her care
braiding the tumbling creek
like daughters' hair.

-Alfred Nicol

Parkland Views

Red fingerprints wiped across the floor,
the farewell gesture of the student,
an orange-size exit hole in her chest
from a cavitating bullet triggered by a
twisted mind let loose.

Surviving students, hands on shoulders,
or hands upraised, parade away from school
single file until they are told to halt.
They know they leave behind another life,
their life and their friends.

Yet from those lives loving faces remain
of teachers, classmates, even janitors.
Young hearts burn to melt battle weapons
into chairs and stools and locker doors.
Machines of death? No more!

Some men who make murder carry no guns
but are murderers nonetheless.
From lecterns of power they herald
the sacred right of guns,
to hide their trade in dead children.

So now the young hearts move to halt
those once-hidden, murderous agendas.

~Bob Brodsky

Reference: *The Atlantic*, February 2018, "What I Saw Treating the Victims from Parkland Should Change the Debate on Guns," by Heather Sher.

About the poet:
Bob Brodsky restores amateur movie film for use in documentaries, film archives, and family histories. With his partner, Toni Treadway, he looks for forgotten gestures.

RobertPBrodsky@gmail.com

Counting the House

Start at the back.
Four from the email list.
Two from the newspaper article.
A librarian doing her own count.
A street person in for the warmth.
Four more from email.
Three friends of the poet, listening intently.
The poet's husband, taking notes.
Four from the high school poetry group.
Three more street people, one listening.
Two staffing the book sales table.
A Boston professor smiling to himself.
The moderator, reviewing her next introduction.
Three of the local poetry elite.
Four of their acolytes, sitting nearby.
The poet, reading a well-known poem.
Don't forget me, counting, not listening.
Not bad for a small town. Thirty-six.

-David Davis

The Umbrella Song

I saw her in the pouring rain,
her hair was plastered to her head,
a red umbrella at her side,
and it is only rain she said.

I saw her in the blinding sun
there were no raindrops in her hair,
her red umbrella at her side
and light was flowing everywhere.

I saw her in the glow of dawn,
her arms drawn tight around her knees,
she put her red umbrella down
and watched the wind blow through the trees.

I miss her in the pale dawn light
that moves across my empty bed,
her red umbrella at my side,
for it is only rain she said.

-David Davis

The Hourglass Range

Love lay in wait but they scared it off,
frightened in return by its doubtful promise
of a cloud-spun world with mountains soft
and sweet melting (even in their first kiss
with other lovers there was pain enough
and dizzy at their feet the great abyss)

Now the present glides by unchanged,
the beat of its heart dull—*time, time,*
quicksand falling on an hourglass range,
untouchable behind crystal blinds.
(It is said in that wilderness love remains,
howling on the barren mountainsides.)

-David Davis

The Coyote*

It sees us as a tolerable source
of dogs and cats it takes back to its den
to feed its young. We possess no force
to keep it in the company of men.
I see one walking proudly in the field.
Its target is a neighbor's garbage can.
It doesn't crouch and wait me out, concealed.
It prefers to show me, if it can,
a dog untamed, no partner in our lives,
no gush of joy if I try to walk near.
Instead it veers toward a hedge and dives
to its side of some ill-defined frontier.
The coyote's not a dog. We took no part
in giving it its independent heart.

-David Davis

* The word "coyote" is pronounced with two syllables in the part of the Western United States where I grew up, and that is the intended pronunciation here.

Redwall Limestone

The ancient standing rock looks down
the canyon. Rafting, we can see
around it shards of flaked debris,
scales discarded as it shaped
itself in time. The sloughed sheets take
their places caught in hip-shot poses,
wearing lichens like pressed roses.

-David Davis
ddavis@vgoassociates.com

About the poet:
David Davis is the Poet in Residence at the Joppa Flats Audubon center, and a member of the Powow River Poets since 2006.

The Fifth

The Mamas and the Papas couldn't really say it
Because the radio wouldn't play it.
Now when we really say it
You can hardly hear it

So your bread crumbs have been scrambled
Hansel and Gretel.
There is nothing back home for you.
Nothing is new back there.

Wait until you see your new bean stalk, Jack
And see where it takes you.
Wherever that is, it won't be where you have been.
There was no joy in being a one-trick pony.

Your GPS has been hacked, Columbus
You were lost anyway
But now are free
To discover new worlds

Always the same questions
What does it mean?
What did you think?
Why did you write this?
It's poetry, we take the fifth

~David Somerset

Bessie

She saw the flowers
beneath the snow
where few cared to look
and none to know

Talked to them
sang to them
loved them
She understood them

They listened to her
heard her
understood her
She meant something to them

Bessie gave her heart away
all she had
a good woman with bad men
a tender soul in a tough world

Bessie died out on highway 61
The same guy who caused her death
stole the money for her headstone
leaving her grave unmarked and forgotten

After many decades a woman appeared
who knew Bessie's music
that music was hers
she loved and sang to those flowers

Janis saw Bessie in her own life
knew her passion
shared her ball and chain
Bessie's heart was hers

Janis bought and placed Bessie's headstone
Not just to mark Bessie's grave
but both of their lives
Remarkable rare lives that
meant something . . . everything

~David Somerset

destruction of Charlottesville, Virginia
Civil War

Blue-Gray Haze

(Written in the wake of Charlottesville and North Korean nuclear threat)

It's a blue-gray haze that descends on today
uncivil war echoes puncture a seam
of post-racial veneers and myopic streams
sunlight washes out and resolves
surreal shadows and lawless scenes
sacking Southern statues and faded dreams
with malice towards some and charity for none
erasing the order of history
to re-litigate yesterday
power politic withholds its police
to promote their spectacle for all to see
coaxing hate from its holes
to join the insane
at play in deadly video games
with unreal savage disdain
in guilt and fear we turn away
from an uneasy time and perilous space
the grass grows a yellow crown
of promises to let us down
but the distraction of destruction
leaves us amorphous, lost and broken
and while we recoil
from an American bad dream
the insects wonder
when they will get their planet back

-David Somerset

Jacob

(We Are All on the Spectrum)

Jacob, digging out your soul
from hearts on hold
In a run-on family
a stolen heart

dream computers
map a universe
with poems that
are themselves poets

artists imagine the unknown
sense the unknowable
their vision over horizons
reveals the hidden within the mist

Jacob, your origin
is not our past
your vision is
not our future

you are many times
what you think
and many more times
what the world knows

they are but half your sky
and few can see you
though brain soldiers guard your gates
your view from those walls is…infinite

–David Somerset

Hidden

souls, easy to lose
ones you would never choose
below your horizon
beneath your feet
out of step
out of reach
edgy, nervous not cool
hearts hanging off of rolled up sleeves
playing your fool
drawn fuzzy in their jagged lines
that blend into shadows, overlooked
hurt and pain hidden in plain sight
outside your lives
but no matter
they are more than you
and they will find each other

-David Somerset

What They Really Needed

He dressed for success
worked hard for five years
stuck in the same job
waited for the next job above him

Worked the hardest
was the most qualified
but he didn't get it
What he really needed was a dog

She went to college for four years
then grad school for two more
running up one hundred and sixty grand
of student debt

only to triumph
in the job market
by landing a ten-dollar-per-hour job at Starbucks
What she really needed was a dog

He spent most of his adult life
looking for someone special
who would stay by his side
love him for who he was

They didn't
they wouldn't
and who ever could?
What he really needed was a dog

Her older sister had
made two attempts

on her own life
but managed to survive

At ten she talked about wanting to die
Her distant parents got her a dog
and they all became emotionally available to that dog
What they had really needed was a dog

pampered, cute, but
disagreeable dog . . .

-David Somerset
calldave123@gmail.com

About the Poet:
Dave is an engineer and IT professional who writes and performs poetry, stories and music. He likes Banksy's idea that "art should comfort the disturbed and disturb the comfortable"; also that truth and good writing converge. Dave's in the MM Anthologies, online sites and his chap book *Among Poets Tonight.*

Alternative Energy

they put a wind turbine in my yard
and promised a whisper of a swoosh
but now my heart beats so hard
I'm going crazy with the whoosh

the bird population is thinning
but sometimes I do see a feather
the blades are so rapidly spinning
their insides don't stay together

the sailors out on Nantucket Sound
don't want no wind mills there
they say put them on solid ground
like maybe Lawrence or Revere

I bought ten thousand gerbils
to spin my electric wheels
I run 'em hard till they're purple
or get blisters on their heels

the oil sheik built a new home
it blocks the moon and stars
at the top is a golden dome
where he tortures electric cars

when Seabrook has its meltdown
everyone will be a bleeder
but not the people living downtown
says the Manchester Union Leader

there's a split in the oil pipeline
somewhere between here and Alaska
Exxon says it wasn't a crime
just another unnatural disaster

the landfills are full of methane gas
grass covers the deadly hill
one might think our energy brass
would just dig instead of drill

she wants to wait till our honeymoon
till I feel some synergy
I asked her are we done so soon
she ran out of energy

-Douglas Lowney

It's About Time

time the scientists can't explain
and the doctors have no cure
accelerating like a runaway train
into a future that's unsure

people with time on their hands
complain they have nothing to do
they just sit and watch the sands
in the hourglass slipping through

PBS runs their charity
where members donate their time
they all get a Roy Orbison CD
and a social hill to climb

a stranger asked me for the time
his clothes worn thin and bare
I said you can have my last dime
but time I have none to spare

when I was cruising into town
I got timed by the traffic cop
just because you gotta slow down
doesn't meant that you have to stop

workers lined up around the block
chain smoking outside the gates
waiting to punch the old time clock
like we used to in the United States

time will give everyone trouble
a battle that we will never win
suddenly your waist is double
and you have an extra chin

it's about time she said to me
you're late again with my check
while driving off in her Infinity
I glance over at my Pinto wreck

time forever will be a mystery
its existence and direction
I look in the mirror what do I see
I see time in my reflection

-Douglas Lowney

Online Dating

I've been lonesome for a while
it comes up most every day
but I'll never walk the aisle
it's too big a price to pay

we all crave love and affection
and I do a lot of reminiscing
when I glance at my reflection
I can see something's missing

my sister-in-law signed me on
she's a hopeless romantic
she forgot that it's foregone
most people I make frantic

faces sweep across the screen
I'm gambling with a losing bet
dangerous is this dating scene
it's safer playing Russian roulette

I fantasize meeting someone
that would give me the hots
a woman who's lots of fun
and has had all her shots

most women on the dating site
seem to love walking the beach
holding hands on a moonlit night
just keeping out of reach

preferring a tall and handsome man
I don't meet the criteria
would they still stick to that plan
marooned in Siberia

she didn't look like her picture
but I know where she got it from
copied from the ancient scripture
of her year book's senior prom

she's actually ninety-nine
but said sixty on the site
I thought she looked just fine
wearing something tight

she's been married three times
then put them all in the ground
never convicted of capital crimes
but I'm not sticking around

I didn't want to drive very far
for just for a casual meet
she said I recognize your car
I live across the street

I met another woman for a drink
some interests hoping to share
it was warm to be wearing mink
and I didn't like the purple hair

she asked if I'm financially secure
I replied well that depends
I can pay if you don't want more
but that's about where it ends

a bow and arrow Cupid shoots
aiming directly at the heart
sometimes it flies other routes
and strikes a different part

online dating didn't work for me
or for anyone else that I've met
but anyway I'm still happy
despite the powerful internet

-Douglas Lowney

Stick 'Em Up

all right your guy won
no need to rub it in thicker
I give up we're all done
scrape off that bumper sticker

soccer mom baby on board
really nobody cares
it looks like her Honda Accord
is badly in need of repairs

this car climbed Mount Washington
coughing in the high thin air
I wonder if it would make it again
they should have left it there

faded stickers are hard to read
it don't matter what they meant
body rot makes the car bleed
but the sticker covers the dent

this car protected by Smith and Wesson
probably true but I'm not scared
I was smart and took a lesson
dealing with the mentally impaired

warning I brake for animals
what about the hoi polloi
no not really just mammals
and the occasional altar boy

my kid beat up your honor student
maybe later dad won't be so proud
it's not going to be that prudent
when he starts firing into the crowd

my other car is a broom
really that's not a shock
I have no pity for her groom
he's a registered warlock

the paw print says dog mom
I bet she's never been bit
when her dog drops a bomb
and her neighbors step in it

my grandson made honor society
me I never cared much for school
I was a bundle of high anxiety
till Marsha joined me in the pool

-*Douglas Lowney*
info@lowneyappraisals.com

About the Poet:
Douglas Lowney lives in Methuen and appraises real estate for his day job. His interests are archery, roller blading, pool, and poetry – now and then.

The Russians Are Coming

America's heartland swung the election
I read the Russians were involved
both coasts made a different selection
it's a crime they don't want solved

Putin is Trump's favorite Kossack
them both being an extrovert
he rides around on horseback
flexing without a shirt

the White House has been condo-ized
the tenants have a foreign accent
being advertised in Prada underlies
the occupant has everything for rent

the Russian Mafia smokes cigarettes
and they like to drink their vodka neat
they torture people with no regrets
then leave them face down on the street

the Russian women working the crops
don't have figures like the ones for sale
their bottoms may resemble their tops
but they can heft a heavy bale

when ordering a Russian mail order bride
be cautious and don't be fickle
or else your body may be found outside
mangled by a hammer and sickle

the Russian subs patrolling our coast
submerged they are out of reach
the sailors savor their periscope post
spying on the girls at the beach

I went to a Russian disco tech
lights flashing blinding my eyes
girls on poles showing what you get
the place crawling with Iranian spies

the Russians have amped up the kicks
to the game of roulette
you pull the trigger and if it clicks
you have won the bet

Russian presence is everywhere
you don't have to leave your car
when you order fast food fare
MacDonald's serves caviar

there's a new family comedy show
they live in the Russian embassy
if you're curious and want to know
you can watch it on W KGB

the fact that the Russians are coming
may not be our biggest fear
with their cheap imports overrunning
the Chinese are already here

-Douglas Lowney

Flag over the Bund, Shanghai
Elizabeth S. Wolf

I raised my hand

and said I, too, was a poet.
We sat at small tables overlooking

The Bund, boats on the water, the red
Chinese flag flapping in the breeze. It was

lunchtime, a poetry panel at the Shanghai
International Literary Festival. The readers

were from Singapore, Mozambique,
Cambridge, Hong Kong. We discussed

history, colonization, how small towns
anywhere in the world are alike, how people

all over the earth need water, shelter, salt,
a mother tongue. At home a storm gathered

up the east coast. At home a high school boy
with a Glock shot two students and died

from his wounds. We don't know who
fired the final shot.

-Elizabeth S. Wolf

Meeting the Host Family

There are smiles all around the table.
Grandma Oma nods, encouraging us all to

eat, eat. Grandpa is still in the kitchen,
still cooking. Grandma approves my

fledgling chopstick skills. I am an American
Polish Latvian Jew, visiting China, where my

Episcopalian WASP Jewish daughter is teaching
English to a 4-year-old German Chinese girl, who is

proudly waving pink plastic chopsticks with
pictures of Peppa Pig, a British cartoon, and crying

"Look at me, look at me!!!" while she stuffs
an entire yummy dumpling into her mouth.

-Elizabeth S. Wolf

Sunset at Mũi Né Vietnam *Elizabeth S. Wolf*

Primate Customs

The nice young Vietnamese scientist
working in the park with pygmy slow loris
could not believe I was travelling solo.
No family? No one to bring with you?
He had a lovely British- accented English
and was clearly concerned.

The next day I checked into a
charming hotel on the beach, on
the South China Sea, just beyond
a fishing village. The room number
was my mother's street address.

I do not believe in coincidence.
I am not travelling alone.

-Elizabeth S. Wolf

Eat the Freaking Marshmallow

I can eat one marshmallow now
or two if I wait. But mama's car
made that scary noise again
and Ray says he can't fix it
without parts, and parts
cost money. So we can have
no money or no car.
I'm going to eat the freaking marshmallow.

I can eat one marshmallow now
or two if I wait. But mama's been
drinking and she called her friend
and they're probably going out, maybe
not coming home tonight.
I don't know what's for dinner.
I'm going to eat the freaking marshmallow.

I can eat one marshmallow now
or two if I wait. But last week
baby got the throw-ups. And then mama
threw up. And then mama lost her job.
Mama is sad and mad and very very
busy 'cept she can't get out of bed.
I'm going to eat the freaking marshmallow.

Well, said the psychologist,
snug in a lab, with a PhD and a
cardigan sweater, like Mr. Rogers;
if only these children could learn
some self-control, they could
pull themselves up by their
bootstraps. That's the problem,
said the white man in a white
coat in a sparkly clean lab (and
who cleans the lab?). These kids need
discipline and strategies for
delayed gratification. It's clear.
It's science. Then he went home
to his own house in a cul de sac
where after dinner and bath and a
game and picture books, he fed his kids
all the rest of the marshmallows.

-Elizabeth S. Wolf
eliz.wolf.z61@gmail.com

About the poet:
Elizabeth S. Wolf's poems have appeared in multiple anthologies & journals. She is the author of two chapbooks: "*What I Learned: Poems*" (Finishing Line Press, 2017) and the 2018 Rattle Chapbook Contest winner "*Did You Know?*" (Summer 2019).

2018 Merrimac Mic Anthology IV wordsmiths
Glowing Awards
March 2018

Not Forgetting

Some things I remember.
A 5-year-old stealing two Silly Puttys
from Woolworths in the hope
that if I gave my brother one,
he wouldn't tell. He did anyway.

Another image comes into view.
The time before cell phones, lost
in a labyrinth of Queens apartments,
knocking on a door answered by
a guy in pajamas. I followed him
to his bedroom for a phone.

Next, I'm canoeing down
the Delaware River, capsizing,
supplies spilling into water
the color of mushrooms, but
hunger drives me to eat the brown-tinged,
fragile bread fragmenting in my fingers,
the soaked, roast beef pale and warm.

My brain ricochets to November 8, 2018,
when I stood on the corner of Rt. 133 and 28,
amid signs of *No One is Above the Law*,
and *Protect Mueller*. Some things
a*re* worth remembering.

~*Gayle C. Heney*
poetryisfun@yahoo.com

About the poet:
A former Poet Laureate of North Andover, artist, and TV producer, this fall Gayle installed sculpture at Maudslay State Park; co-edited the poetry book *Soulmates*; displayed artwork at the Nevins Library and Whistler House Museum of Art; and produced "No Gas Poetry."

For Haley

The dogs are strangely silent.
Golden-brown eyes wide
as if disbelieving, tails tucked,
the click of their nails on the tile.

The dogs are strangely silent.
Women whispering between vases
of pink roses. Among the ferns,
Mary pale in her porcelain glow.

The dogs are strangely silent.
Overflowing dish drainer, buttery
cakes clogging counters, coffee brewing
few will drink, piles of paper products.

The dogs are strangely silent.
Red-eyed friends, family hugging,
tissues, lots of tissues. A crown
of flowers in a Facebook picture.

The dogs are strangely silent.
Someone's eating gingerbread
as fingers fuss with plastic wrap,
wrapping, unwrapping, rewrapping.

The dogs are strangely silent.
So many pale faces
in a crowded home
tasting disbelief.

~Gayle C. Heney

Banyan tree
Chennai, India
like a poet, extending its aerial roots
Isabell VanMerlin

Half Full

Yahrzeit glass, half-depleted,
Replenished with memories,
The not-forgotten but less bereft,
Mortality's debris noted by its absence.

Living flame, a slow dance,
No breath, no breeze,
Perhaps a presence,
Transitory visitor,
Or one who never left,
The journey not completed.

-Harris Gardner
tapestryofvoices@yahoo.com

Originally appeared in *Ibbetson Street* #43

About the poet:
Harris Gardner's credits: *The Harvard Review*; *Midstream*; *Fulcrum*; *Chest*; *Ibbetson Street* - 2010 to present; co-founder Tapestry of Voices and Boston National Poetry Month Festival with Lainie Senechal.

Stop Signs

What chapter have you adopted
In life's voluminous tome?
If not, then what page is yours to own?
Not even a paragraph! Surely, at least a line!
Come on, then. At least a period
At the end of your complex sentence.
Ai, Ai! Not even a pen's pin point;
At least you deserve a semi-colon.
All right, you tough negotiator,
I shall, perforce, settle for a comma.
A pause is better than finis.
At the end, perhaps a beginning.
The cycle, a circle.

A serpent with its tail in mouth.
You, mounted on a wheel
That gains momentum.
You cling, in panic,
Bouncing down a mountain.
At the bottom is a hewn barrier.
You close your eyes and pray.
Somewhere, God listens and makes
A brief entry in the book.

-Harris Gardner

Originally appeared in *Ibbetson Street* #41

Unwanted

Originally appeared in *Ibbetson Street*, #42

The world is pregnant
With a strange, ill-boding child.
The fetus in the womb is Want.
Who had such cojones
To make the planet enceinte?

When this abandoned babe is born,
Who will still its ravenous craving?
When it weeps, who, then will claim this cub?
Parentage unknown, or a multitude,
None will call it their own.

Is it a dybbuk that swims in the prenatal sea
That harbors no future serenity?
The world's womb nears full-term.
Its size may portend contentious twins:
Another Cain and Abel, 2.0 light, or heavy water,
Or a Jacob and Esau simulacrum.

Perhaps transgressing Nephilim
Or maybe multiple miracle births.
Will a great shofar blast, heard
'Round the wobbled, hobbled globe
Announce a saving presence
To nullify want as only a false rumor?

If not this pressing need,
Pushing against restraining walls,
Then what in its stead??
What fatherless/motherless being
Will emerge with none signing up to nurture?

Ocean waves shiver the shore;
Guardians of *tikun olom* are en route.
Summon the midwives, Shifra and Puah;
Pray for a positive outcome
To this worrisome conundrum.

-*Harris Gardner*

Delete, Delete!

Scrolling down the numbers,
I seek to eliminate those now
Obsolete. The first on the chopping
Block is shaded in blue. I press clear
And a query appears: "Do you wish
To delete this entity?" I knew it!
These gremlins do exist! My disbelieving
Eyes correct the question: "Do you wish to delete
This entry?" Much more mystery were the entity
There. That would solve the universal enigma
Of electronics that seem to be endowed
With free will, their erratic behavior
When they won't adhere to our daily demands.
No virus interferes, at least not now; however,
No relief charges to the rescue to lift the siege
And cure the cosmic cell phone addiction.
Press delete Take care how you dictate
Your heavy-handed commands.

-Harris Gardner

Originally appeared in *Ibbetson Street* #40

Acknowledgment

Be sure to thank Mrs. Campbell for the ride.
Yes, Momma-
Did you thank Mrs. Campbell for the ride?
Yes, Momma-
Yes, Momma-
YES, MOTHER.
Age 4 this started. I was a 2-year kindergarten student.
Mother was desperate to get me out of the house.
She brought me up right, though.
To be polite.
She was born on the cusp of Virgo/Libra
And she was thorough; thank you, Virgo.
She passed that on to me, too.
It always sounds good in an interview:
"Yes, I'm detail-oriented."
But they don't like it when you actually DO
pay attention to details.
It takes too much time.
We don't actually WANT the customer
to know everything about their account.
Follow the script. To the LETTER and DOT.
A lot of people are lazy, don't want to be thorough
don't know how to be
wouldn't be even if they knew how to be.
Too much trouble. Costs too much. Waste of time.
And would you be thanked
for doing a good, thorough job?
Probably not. That's *my* rant.

Almost everyone on the planet uses gas.
Where would we be without it? Dark ages?
And this situation wasn't intentional;
it was a mistake; a step missing in the procedure
of replacing some old with new. . . . .
of course.

Has anyone ever thanked Columbia Gas
for delivering such a great source
of energy and power?
Maybe they would have thought about
the people they were serving
how they were appreciated
and how this great and powerful energy source
could be very destructive and deadly
if not controlled properly, safely.
Maybe.
It's a thought.

I swear to you, every single afternoon when I came
running into the house, my mother would ask me,
Did you thank Mrs. Campbell for the ride?
I always answered Yes, because I always did.
To this day it is my intention to thank people,
acknowledge them,
as often as possible.
I truly believe it is one of the most important things
to do when living on a planet as we do here.
It's as important as gas.
It's a necessity – for survival.

I think it helps
to believe in reincarnation.
Maybe we'll get it right next time
if . . .

~Isabell VanMerlin

reference: On September 13, 2018, excessive pressure in natural gas lines owned by Columbia Gas caused a series of explosions and fires which occurred in as many as 40 homes, with over 80 individual fires, in the Merrimack Valley, Massachusetts, towns of Lawrence, Andover and North Andover. One person was killed; 30,000 forced to evacuate.

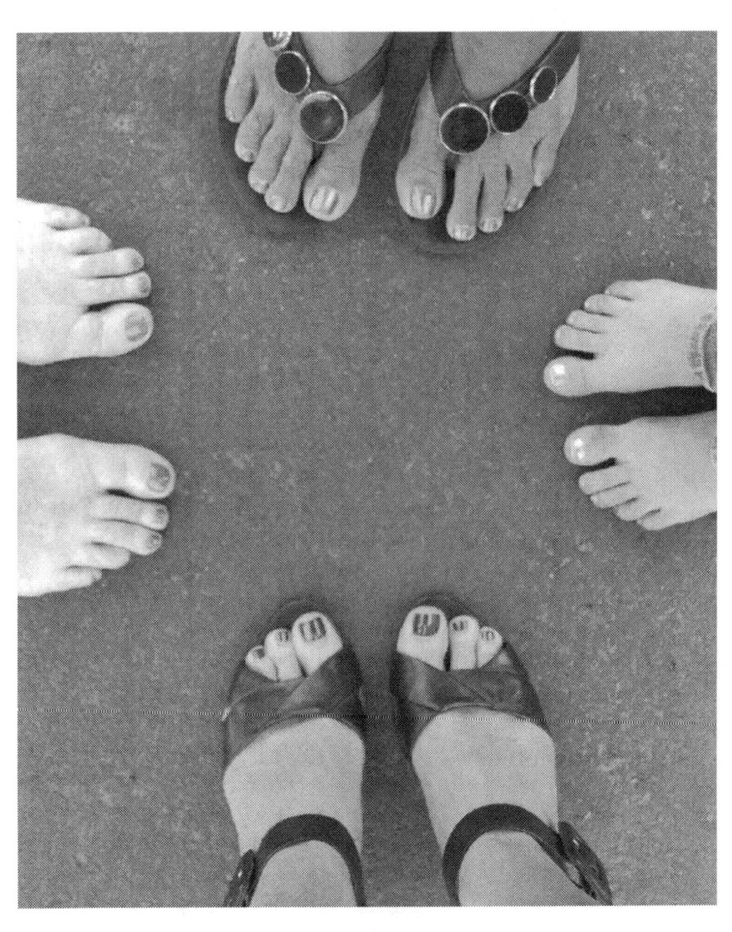

After pedicures, Isabell VanMerlin
from 12 o'clock, clockwise: Mina, Reyna, Sia, Isabell

Point Your Toes

"Now, point your toes."
When do they say that?
And who is the 'they' that says that?
I know they say that
when you are learning to dive
and maybe when you're doing
the hokey pokey.

And what do they tell you to do
with your arms when you're
learning to dive? I don't remember
anything about my arms.

The orthopedic guy
was telling me how we learn
to walk: heel > toe, heel>toe -
but when our joints start going
we lean forward – don't have our hips under us -
and it messes up the joints even more.
Maybe we should walk
toe > heel, toe > heel
or would that be only
if we're walking backwards?

Maybe you point your toes
when you dance the minuet
Is it rude to point your toe
at someone
like pointing your finger
at someone is rude?

I think it's probably impossible
to point your toes when you do
a back dive. Which way
would they point?

Since we don't have tails
would we try to chase
our pointed toes?

Pointing your toes seems like
a good thing, though. Stretching
your fee, ankles, arches, insteps-
precise, intentional; making a point!

How often do we point our toes?
Do you notice?
Would anyone notice?
Birds seems to point their toes
AND their legs when they fly.

How about when we ascend
from this mortal plane?
Would anyone notice?
Would anyone remember us
for pointing our toes?

~Isabell VanMerlin

Seagulls on the Beach

haiku

seagulls on the beach
scavenging – well – having lunch
low tide in summer

white grits, black pepper
no just seagulls on the beach
regular beach bums

looking into wind
next storm will bring tasty bites
seagulls on the beach

~Isabell VanMerlin

About Contrasts

I like to see ice on ponds
white in the winter
in New England

And I like to see ice on the edge
of ponds with the water in the middle
dark and moving – not frozen

I like the contrast

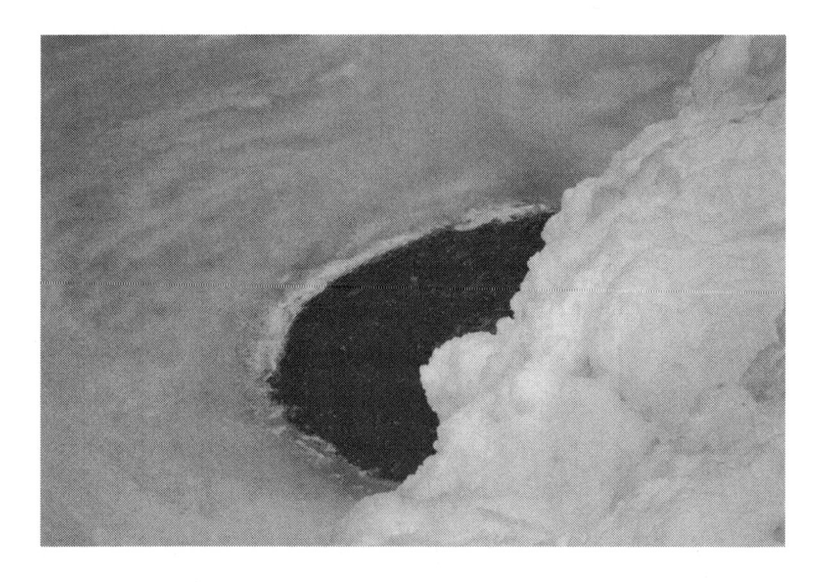

Skin can be white
on the outside
who knows what color
is inside?

There's no light inside our earthsuits
our blood and bodily
juices and parts
could be any color – like black -
with no light.

What about the beach
on a hot summer day?
The biting cold wind of
a nor'easter in winter

I like the beach *any* time of year

and what about the contrast
between safe and dangerous?
Who makes up that stuff?

Contrast heightens perception
and experience

Comparison is the cause of all unhappiness.

-Isabell VanMerlin

A Dawning
tanka

the light comes softly
gently defining cacti
round and spikey spines
caressing, teasing eyelids
beginning to shape my day

-Isabell VanMerlin

isabell@isabellvanmerlin.com

About the poet:
Isabell VanMerlin started Merrimac Mic five plus years ago [holy smokes] because she couldn't get to Speak Up! in Lynn, MA, anymore, having moved farther and farther north. As long as the words keep flowing along the Merrimac River she'll be content– more than that– *happy* to hear your words!

Breccia

A ship, they said: an island's more the case.
One touch of lips that tore four souls apart.
The clock has stopped above the campus lawn.
What matters most can hang you from a chain.

Three sets of feet were splashing in the foam.
Above canals, the windows cut the sun.
And there you are in photo number three.
You started skidding sideways on the road.

He leaves a candle where the future died.
There still are things that he can never say.
That grey flypaper will not let her go.
But nothing here exists that won't be gone.

The rubber mask, the hiss of oxygen.
Outside the silent river rumples by.

-J. Knowles

2009 Superhighway Contest

drops

stepping on a dead branch
...it crackles

a drop of water
shakes on a twig-tip
eye on a stalk
blinking

a camera with a copy
of the world in its belly
...a taunting perfection
focused but too tiny to enter

a spark of sun is shining from an edge
bent into a crescent moon
through a loom of imaged stems

the drop falls in a blink

fog off the pond is still climbing the hill
other drops growing, are waiting to see
and eat the world
to fall and split
to wick into the earth
again

~J. Knowles

keeping watch

it's saturday, and a rocky beach...
i feel strong enough to smile now
though this smile is a scaffolding of vanity
an open lattice wanting the skin of proof
or perhaps vines of desire, to cover, to justify

here we are by a concrete shoreline
a sweeping scimitar of progress
looking inland to plateaus of contentment
divided by canyons of mishap

for now, the stars of tragedy are fading
above an ice cream stand, and we are busy
marshalling sweet drips of distraction
with tongues that can't complain right now

is this existence,
this struggle to stay ahead
just a tire-pressed squirrel
caught between two tugging gulls
under a lingering moonless night

we should spend some time now
back to back, resting against each other
keeping an eye out all around,
talking about these days
...keeping watch

~J. Knowles

Luxury You Can Afford

Down the aisle from me,
In the WalMart pharmacy,
A tall elderly woman in a
Bright red dutchboy haircut
Stares at an old puddle of
Pricey skin treatment
From a broken bottle.

She leans down, smiles, stabs a long red fingernail
Into the puddle. It cuts cleanly.
She slits the dried skin, folds it open to the left.

She rotates her wrist, shovels a load of
Moisturizer onto the fingernail. It piles up well.
She smiles more broadly. Everything is saying
This wants to happen.

She dots the creme on her face in six places,
Forehead, cheeks, and chin, rubs the drops in slowly
with both hands.
She stares at the ceiling, tuning in to the sensation.
"Mmmm," she says, "Mmmm."

-J. Knowles

In *Durable Goods,* March 2010

Neon Love

(spoken over instrumental loop from Beach House, "Beyond Love")

There is a time sometimes, your lonely gloom
Is pierced ...you see a face across the room.
She will flash, illuminated from above...
You're suddenly so empty: I call that *neon love.*

{ chorus: Neon Love}

I've been sending out my signals:
does that light the dash in you?

{Neon Love}

I've been fully charged but static
since your grille came rolling through.

{Neon Love}

<<VACANCY>>...my...<<VACANCY>>
I flash into your night.

{Neon Love}

I'll take in your trends and tendencies;
my arms and rooms are warm and bright.

{Neon Love}

I ask now where am I, now that I can't see you?
You left and broke my compass, now my bearing isn't true.
The tubes that light my heart are cold; the current won't pass through.

{Neon Love}

So you must touch my skin to let the current in, this *neon love.*

{Neon Love}

I need need need need your *neon love.*
(I'll put a mint on every pillow)

{Neon Love}

I need need need need your *neon love.*
(should I give and freeze beneath the weeping willow?)

{Neon Love}

I need need need need your *neon love.*

-J. Knowles

The Grapes

For weeks I smelled wild Concords,
Below the power lines.

The scent was strong, and shifted,
From juice, to mold, to wine,

And when the leaves had fallen,
The grapes were hanging still.

I thought the birds would eat them.
Perhaps next year, I will.

-J. Knowles
jameskathome@gmailcom

About the poet:
Jim Knowles won the 2009 Poetry Superhighway Contest, and placed second in the 2010 Inkwell Poetry Competition; is President and MC at the Frost Foundation; published a few fun tomes at blurb.com; and is in a Mass. poets' collection by Neils Kjaer (Denmark), with Frost, Dickinson, and Crapsey.

Mist, watercolor
Lainie Senechal

Mist

A fine mist settles
over a lake that does
not stir from slumber -
a lazy, meditative moment.
Today's deluge of rain
will nourish landscape,
fill rivers whose flow
will flood to rapids,
while the waning moon
lies hidden behind clouds.
For now, no storms to brave,
Only a slight breeze which
murmurs in the bare branches.

~Lainie Senechal

Beach Plums

In last melancholy moments of summer,
tenuously balanced on a border:
departure of season's long languid hours,
arrival of preparations and uncertainty
where air has cooled but sun still warms.
Now picking beach plums -
red-purple fruit, perfectly round,
color of late evening's last light,
smaller than a cherry but
bigger than a blueberry,
on a tree, diminutive and gnarled,
with gray, lichen-laced branches
on back edge of dune.
It has weathered winter winds,
blowing sand and salt spray
to produce an abundance,
too sour to eat, so jelly is made.
Bounty boiled down to
a deep garnet-hue liquid
that shimmers like a jewel
in its clear crystal jar.
The taste, wild and plummy,
decidedly not domesticated
with a hint of sea air.
Autumn brings renewed tasks,
but after indolence of long light,
I am not at all prepared

and can only focus
on the harvest of beach plums
to bring the memory of summer's sun,
something shiny and sweet,
into the darkening days.

~*Lainie Senechal*
emsenechal@gmail.com

Published in *Ibbetson Street #43,* June 2018,
Ibbetson Street Press, Somerville, MA

About the poet:
Lainie Senechal, artist and former poet laureate of Amesbury, MA, has read and featured at many venues in New England. Her poetry has appeared in journals and anthologies. She co-authored two poetry volumes and authored a recent chapbook, *Vocabulary of Awakening.*

Haiku

Tinkling of chimes heard
Above whispering breezes
Through bare-limbed willow.

Grassless moss green lawn
Squirrel scratches searching for
Buried winter food.

Unmarked brown boxes
Stacked high, fill an old attic
Memories long past.

Colored salt shaker
Sits on kitchen windowsill
Waiting for dinner.

Wooden fence posts rot
Frozen winter snow and rain
Destroy barriers.

Rusting metal door
Impenetrable barrier
Between cold and warmth.

Damaging winds howl,
Blow down trees, wooden houses
Before moving on.

Twisting winds threaten
Touch down, carry away homes,
Dreams gone; build again.

Delicate snowdrops,
First blossoms in early spring,
Promise warmer days.

A leafy willow
Breeze sways branches in the wind
Crushed roots bring it down.

Young trees, old trees stand
Together against the wind
As the storm passes.

Red and white tulips,
One living, one machine made,
Bloom in a garden.

~Louise Hart
louisehart@email.com

About the poet:
Louise Hart has been publishing and published since age 13.

Following in Father's Shadow

As I walk his path and stand where
He once surely did, I wonder, maybe
He would have gone anyway. Who
Knows? I shall go. We all do.
I always thought that I would hit
The wall running, driving as fast
As I could, pedal pressed to the floor,
But that is for the very young who,
If not snatched like a budding flower,
Would never go. After full blossom,
Stately tall tulip, iris, crowning rose
Endure the insults of nature, eating,
Browning, tearing away triumphs,
Treasures earned, stored and displayed.
Petals fall off. First one, then another,
And another until only the stamen,
Pulp, stem and leaves are left.
Even they with the glory and
All beauty gone, bow and bend
Until crushed by the sting of unseen
Night frost in October. It deepens
In November killing all that grew
In the family's seasonal garden.
Leaves are raked, gathered, piled,
Burned, mulched or buried, soon
Forgotten under snow. Next year
A totally different crop will grow
In their stead. Passersby are unlikely
to give thought or know the difference.

-Louise Hart

On Hearing August Leaves

The shushing, drying leaves
In a light mid-August breeze
Whisper autumn's in the offing.
Her entrance is not far away.

With breathless humidity
July spent summer's heat
Boiling it like tea water
In a screeching kettle.

Fiery heat sparked lightning that
With thunderous roar announced
The imploding, exploding of
Seasons pushing in, pushing out.

Life's ever changing; leaves
But buds a few short months ago
With brown and yellow tips
Sing in anticipation of letting go

In a voice so soft, the melody
All but eludes me as I listen
For the end of the chorus before
The final verse is sung.

~Louise Hart

Threat

I am going to destroy the world.
It won't take too much effort.
I just need to live my life
the same way I've always lived it.
This plan might take a while.
I may not live long enough
to see the fruits of my labors.
But no matter —
There are plenty of others
who will continue my work
after I am gone.
And when we are finished,
Not a single human being
will be left alive.
We are going to destroy the world.
I dare you to try and stop us.

-Matthew Cockreham

The inspiration for this poem comes from the realization that in order to address a global crisis, one must first acknowledge one's own role in the perpetuation of the crisis, even if that role is passive.

January Afternoon

A sun-drenched love seat
A book of good poetry
Bring it on, winter

-Matthew Cockreham
matt_cockreham@yahoo.com

About the poet:
Matthew Cockreham enjoys photography, birding, nature walks, local food, spending time outdoors, and exploring creativity in all its forms. Poetry is the latest in his series of experiments in artistic expression, and he is thankful to Merrimac Mic for their encouragement and support!

Mammatus Clouds

Thunder, lightning, rain,
Is it the end of the world?

I feel like my body is floating
In space, maybe because I am
Watching this from my fourth
Floor condo.

The weather rumbles like a car
Having trouble starting.

I think of other storms; I watch,
I listen, I may have to drive
Eventually to a meeting.
Scientists say that you are safest
In your car, during an electrical storm.

Rumble, rumble, I put on the television
To listen to the weather on the news
And a car advertisement comes on:
"Power for the Pro."

Thunder and more thunder,
Can I fly off my deck like Batwoman?
To save the people lost in this storm?

The weatherman talks about possible hail,
meanwhile the thunder sounds
Like bombs exploding,
and the weatherman continues with chances of
Tornadoes and shows mammatus
Clouds in the sky, omens of
h

Dark clouds, thunder continues and
Lighting lights the sky
I give up; I am not going to the meeting.

~Muriel Angelil
mm36angelil@gmail.com

About the poet:
Muriel Angelil is a prolific artist in several media, showing, reading, presenting in New England, and is about to publish her latest collection of poems, *justsaying*. She lives and works in Amesbury, MA.

Snow by Muriel Angelil

First Snow

Milk, potatoes, eggnog,
Supermarket lines are full
Express checkout
A friend talks over coffee
Of thanksgiving dinner
Memories of past holidays,
Falling snow accumulates
The wipers dance with the
Music from the radio
Carrying groceries to the
Front door, treading slowly
On the slippery sidewalk,
Broken elevator means
Climbing stairs to fourth floor.
A glass of eggnog, as falling
Snow covers my purple mums
In the planter on my deck.
Outside the plow makes a path
For the cars; inside it's quiet, too
Quiet, even though it's cozy and warm.
I put on my parka, scarf and Uggs
To cross the street to my studio
Determined to create something
New and beautiful this first snow.

-Muriel Angelil

Fog installation sculpture by Fujiko Nakaya
Emerald Necklace, Boston, fall 2018
Muriel Angelil

Lost Time

If time is lost is there a place
Where it can be found?
If I am daydreaming am I
Losing time? Or is time
Sitting still?
Sometimes time drifts away
So slowly I feel like the hand
On the clock has stopped moving.
When time flies is there a special
Place it goes or like a butterfly
It lands on another person to create
Happiness and more happiness?

Actually *time* is an invented word
By people who have watches,
Clocks and iPhones and who need
To be anchored to this earth.
But we creative people like to
Daydream, space out, and for us
Time does not exist.
How can an esoteric word like
Time define my life or yours?

I believe that lost time travels to
Places where it is welcomed by
People who are always "on time."

-Muriel Angelil

My Past

My past is familiar and unfamiliar
At the same time,
It is the story of another person
Even another place.
I see myself as shy and insecure
But with an undercurrent of
A driving force,
A force that propelled me forward
To forego home and native land
And to lay roots in an unknown
Earth, in a soil moist with hope
And fertile for new seeds.
I may have had plans, and goals
Helped me move forward to an
Uncertain present and future.
I took the untrodden road and
Tasted the atmosphere and
Language of a new land. I thrived;
I sprouted new seeds, that grew
Into children and grandchildren.
I drew maps of my past and
Present and they became paintings
That I showed and exhibited.
I don't really know why I chose
This path but I am glad that I did.

-Muriel Angelil

Shimmering Waves on PI Dawn
acrylic on canvas, PD Turco

Shimmer

Sun rays shimmer in the air.
Time melts as foam-topped waves crash down
on sparkling sand out to the pier.
Sun rays shimmer in the air.
At high tide castles disappear.
A child's towel becomes a gown.
Sun rays shimmer in the air.
Time melts as foam-topped waves crash down.

~ Paulette Demers Turco

Poem first appeared in chapbook, *In Silence*, by PD Turco, published by Finishing Line Press, June 2018.

Almost Overnight in Tuam

1970's

They stumbled in a pile of baby bones
and skulls whose eyeless faces stared at them
as if remembering beyond the wall.
The two boys dropped the apple cores, ran home
so fast, their legs could hardly carry them.
Their story jumbled, mom and dad believed them,
warned them, "You boys, never go back! Never!
Never." They couldn't help it. Something drew them—

maybe the sound of large equipment rumbling.
This change happened almost overnight?
The apple trees were gone, new grass was laid,
the blue of Holy Mary's mantle glistening
in a grotto. Trace of cracked concrete,
hidden alabaster bones—gone.

Tuam, Ireland, is where the St. Mary's Mother and Baby Home existed from 1925 -1961, overseen and funded by the Irish government and Catholic Church. This poem is part of a developing series. (Tuam pronounced: Chowm)

~ *Paulette Demers Turco*

Poem first published in Ibbetson Street Press, # 44, 2018.

Rage on the Third Floor

A city outside Boston, 2015

photo: *Ajar*
PD Turco

He bludgeoned her one year ago, then fled
though killed by cops responding to the scene—
the 911 call by the oldest son.
The bat the father used, exhibit A,
put mother in a coma for two months,
the kids all sent away to foster homes.
Most hits were to her head. He'd thought her dead
so left the house, she sprawled, alone until
the kids came home to find her on the floor,
blood pooled and wet. They saw. They saved her life—
she's blind, she limps, she's tired and she forgets.
Her PCA is with her every day—
just four hours: to wash, make meals, give meds.
She falls a lot, but now she feels she's safe.

~ Paulette Demers Turco

Poem first published in *Ibbetson Street Press* #43, 2018.

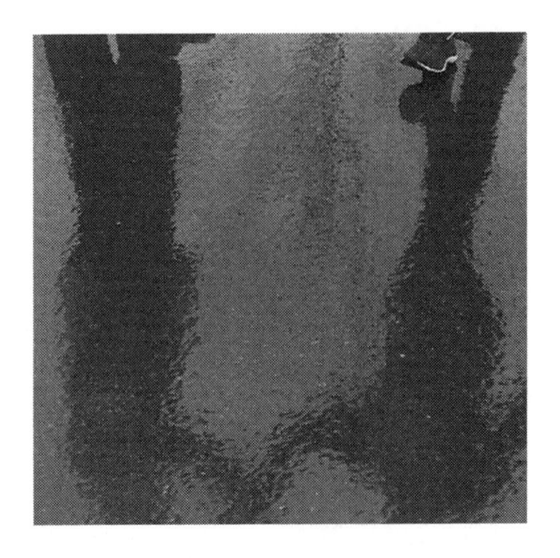

Photo: *Rain Shadows*, PDTurco

Plunge

Raindrops plunge through glistening air;
in streaks of mist, they soak the ground
creating cloaks of haze and glare.
Raindrops plunge through glistening air
as tulips break through soil, once bare,
and children's boots splash puddled ground.
Raindrops plunge through glistening air;
in streaks of mist, they soak the ground.

~ *Paulette Demers Turco*
pdturco@msn.net

Poem first appeared in chapbook, *In Silence*, by PD Turco.

About the poet:
Turco's poetry appears in *The Lyric*, *Ibbetson Street Press*, *Merrimac Mic Anthologies II, III, and IV*, and *In Silence*, her first chapbook, published by Finishing Line Press, June 2018. She is a member of the Powow River Poets and is an MFA candidate at Lesley University, Cambridge, MA.

Enough Doubt ?

To Choose a Judge

If he can't remember,
maybe he was drunk.
Some boasted of his
drinking in the high
school yearbook,
not before the senators of course—his hands
revealed a nervous twitch with this new line of questions.

She's been trying to forget, remembers all
too well, as it derailed her path for years. Just follow
her sudden change of habits, worries of her friends.

If it's a man, a judge, a cop, he is believed.

He could have a motive— tell a lie, mislead,
especially in regard to sex, the forced, rejected
kind. If he was drunk, you wouldn't be surprised
when he says he can't remember such a time?

But chances are, it wasn't just this time, maybe
other girls.... if he believed, adults around him
thought boys will be boys, especially handsome ones
boasting in the football team's locker room.

If she snuck into the nearest bathroom when
she escaped his grip, and pulled herself together,
snuck out, fearful she'd be found out, not
believed or worse than that, accused of wanting this.

She knew the rules were different for the high school girls
on weekends while their moms and dads would dine

out at the Country Club or theatre, symphony,
when family liquor cabinet keys were found.
Who bought the kegs of beer…a hero then?

He's climbing high—the ladder of success.

She has in other ways, in science, research labs,
integrity a part of every day, in journals,
at universities, but does that measure up?

How many liars pass a lie detector test
at the FBI? Would he risk taking one?
Do lies matter for this high court nominee?

Senators want their candidate to be approved,
become the highest judge, and should she disappear
into the shadows, what's to say of character
for senators to judge? Would Solomon agree?

What about his boasting in his Georgetown Prep
yearbook: His 100 kegs. What of his statement
on a graduation stage just weeks ago:
"What occurs at Georgetown Prep, stays at Georgetown
Prep." Are those the words of justice in a judge?

Where does she go, now she's the named accuser?
Why must she hide—in fear, her forced into the limelight,
to live that hour again and all the repercussions?

Senators vote will be without the information
needed to choose the wisest judge. He'll fill the seat.

Integrity is not the bar they wish to reach.

~Paulette Demers Turco

Lost Keys Found

I found an old key ring
That I had lost years ago

It was under the inside flap
Of an old ratted and tatted tour pack

That I had left in my friend's garage

I looked at the keys
On the key ring

One: Was to A house
in a town

Where I no longer live.

Two: Was to my old truck
That was broke down and towed

And I never retrieved

Three: Was to a Harley
I sold too cheap

During the divorce.

Four: Was for a mail box
I no longer rent.

Five: Was to a shed
Where now
her Mr. Right

Keeps his Bike.

Six: Was to a tool box
That was stolen

While I was homeless.

I look at the keys
On the key ring
again

And say to myself ...

"WOW!"

"This must be
my lucky day!"

-K. Peddlar Bridges
laconia1916@yahoo.com

About the poet:
K. Peddlar Bridges, aka The Roadpoet, is a writer and poet living in Laconia, NH. Peddlar rides a Harley, has a degree from Harvard Extension School and is the current Poet Laureate and Historian of *Laconia Motorcycle Week.* He has hosted 100+ cable TV shows and has six books on Amazon.

Classical Man

The curve of your back is exposed
in the steel-cold light, enfolded
in a generic cotton robe
printed with blue boats
riding between snaps
and ties that don't hold.

There's a tremor in the sheet
from your arm, drawn taut
by your hand's squeeze, grasping
for relief from the *bees*
caught inside you, stinging
all the way to your feet.

I hear the sounds of rubber soles
squeaking on mirror-like floors,
along with the metronome tick
of drips dripping through the night,
and muffled voices drifting
through the half-opened door.

When I step into the hall
I see a print on the wall—
columns in a classical scene,
with a statue of a man,
his torso sinewy and tall;
perfect, until his fall.

I imagine him in an arena,
brave, in a contest of strength,
before grievous wounds would
damage his youthful, marble limbs
and he'd have to give up the fight.
I return to your room…and wait.

~Priscilla Turner Spada

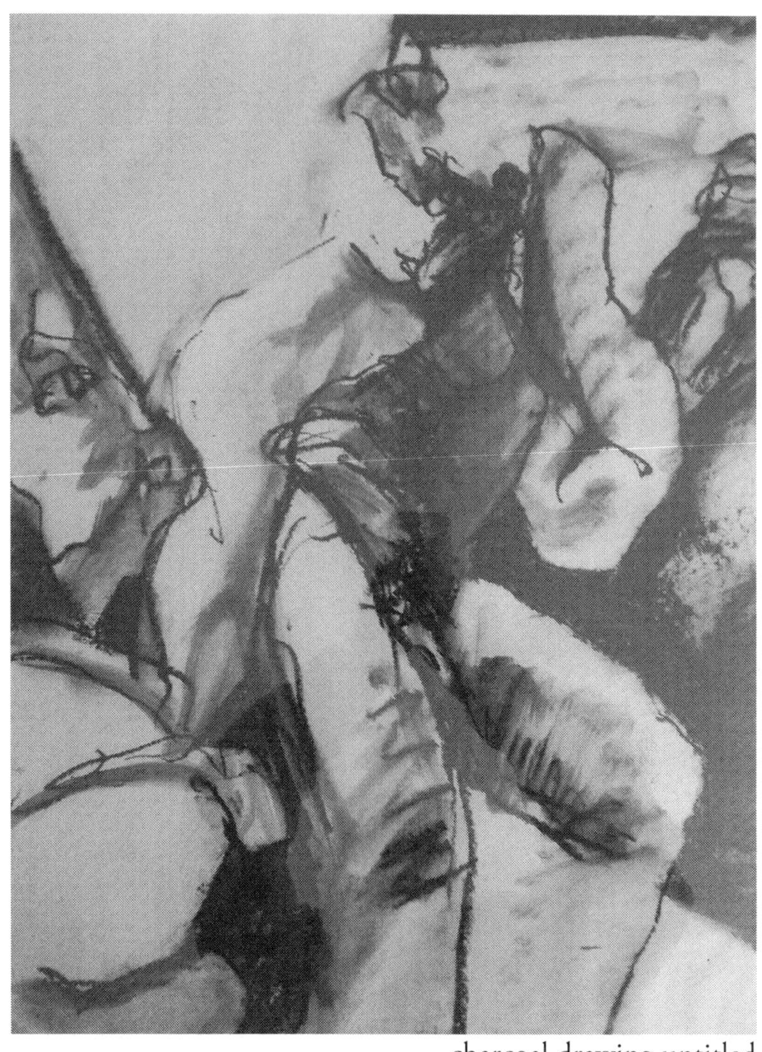

charcoal drawing untitled
-Priscilla Turner Spada

photograph *Button Collection*
Priscilla Turner Spada

Buttons

This button's from two-of-a-kind.

This button's for a baby's shoe.
This button's colored pink, not blue.

This button's for a pinafore.
This button's for the pants she tore.
This button's from the mitt she wore.

This button's for her yellow coat.
This button's to pin up a note.
This button's for the schoolbook tote.
This button's to promote a vote.

This button's for a button-down.
This button's for her blue ballgown.
This button is sequined and round.
This button starts the Limo to town.
This button tore off, caused a frown.

This button's for her alarm clock.
This button's for her fancy sock.
This button's to press down and talk.
This button will undo the lock.
This button's for her artist's smock.
This button's for her wedding frock.

This button's made of mother-of-pearl.
This button's made just for a girl.
This button has a carved-in curl.
This button's from a wooden burl.
This button has a twist and swirl.

This button's yellow, pink and green.
This button's shaped like a jellybean.
This button's from her daughter's jeans.
This button's polished to a sheen.

This button's for a tattered sleeve.
This button's for the warp and weave.
This button's so she'll never leave.

This button has a lot of stitches.
This button reflects her many riches.

This button's from two-of-a-kind.

-Priscilla Turner Spada
priscillarts@comcast.net

About the poet:
Priscilla Turner Spada, Newburyport, MA, has a chapbook, *Light in Unopened Windows,* Finishing Line Press. Her poems, artwork, beads and jewelry are in numerous books: *Merrimac Mic Anthology II - IV; Ibbetson Street 40 - 44; Lark Books*. She has read and featured at many regional events.

watercolor *Up Country*
Priscilla Turner Spada

Blue Twilight

A row of houses tucked beside the woods,
related by their stark simplicity,
can't be really called a neighborhood.
But shoveled paths reveal that somebody,
like old-man Shaw, has done the work, and could
be settled in beside these quiet trees.

The indigo and mauve of dusk's cool light
shroud the hills beyond and come in close,
bringing on the crisp New Hampshire night,
enveloping the snow-sharp roofs and road.

The icy crust of night steals in; all's still.
Then coyotes echo in the distant hills.
Cats and chickens, lambs, are safe within.
A rifle's propped against the barn's grain bin.

-Priscilla Turner Spada

After

After one has been
starving long enough,
hunger subsides;
only weakness remains,
yielding to cold,
ending with heart failure.

I am no longer
dreaming of you.
Once the dream
fades away...
...it never was.

~ *R. A. Whelan*
RockportPoetry@gmail.com

About the poet:
R. A. Whelan is a poet, playwright, and essayist who lives in Rockport, MA. His poems intend to be mirrors of everyday events that reflect more universal themes. His dogs, cats, goats, chickens and bees could care less about that. He has four awesome children and five fantastic grandchildren.

Authenticity Assassinated

The lightning bolt has struck the tree
Splitting it
Toppling its tall arrogance
Scattering songbirds
Green leaves parachute like kisses
Intended for the heart

Self-consciousness remains
Like false teeth
Abandoned in a jar
The mouth anonymous
Buried and forgotten
Still searching for words

Days of continuous rain
The flood of hopeless
Waiting for water lilies
Blooming in the desert
Lighting up
To be seen by the blind

It began with the simple desire
To be the thought that comes
Suddenly into your day
With the sweet weight
Of wildflowers and starlight
Making you unexpectedly happy

~ R. A. Whelan

Cracked

Poets are crazy.
Philosophers are crazy.
I am doomed… being both.
But I think the crazy came first.
That state of mind that steps
Out of the common-sense reality
Into the uncommon,
The not usually seen,
Yet almost always felt.
It renders an experience
Of not quite fitting
Which enables the pattern
To be undeniably observable
Like the piece of broken color
In a stained glass window
That allows you to see the sun.

~ *R. A. Whelan*

Do Birds Die?

Do birds die?
They must… it's just
You never see their corpses
Except perhaps
When ravaged by a cat
Or the occasional one
That tried to fly
Through a clean closed window
Lying neck broken on the porch
Or had misjudged traffic
And was left bloody and twisted on the road

They must generally die in midflight
And disintegrate before hitting the ground
Their feathers swept away by the wind.

The other night
Like some suicide bomber
Wrapped in a vest of explosive self pity
I hurled spasmodic false threats
Detonated words like a terrorist
Oblivious to consequences
Only to destroy myself
And damage an innocent
The innocent who gives
The world its meaning.

Now
Every day since
I wish that instead
I was some bird that died in midflight
And disintegrated before hitting the ground.

~ *R. A. Whelan*

He Is So Quiet

He is so quiet
And keeps his distance

He is a carpenter
Who makes fine things
With patient calloused hands

Known him for years

Many times I've tried
To make some conversation
But to no avail

When his brother died
I felt his loss
But had no words
To break the isolation

Such great devouring grief
In empty searching eyes
Betraying a wandering heart
And a cavernous soul

There is a lighthouse
In some restless ocean
That speaks for him

He's so very quiet
And keeps his distance

~ *R. A. Whelan*

I Am Time Itself

I am time itself

I thinks it is
Me
Me thinks it is being

There was being before I
But Me had no memory
There was no time

Then I became
And so did time
Which only passes
While I is

Awake

Time appears
Wanting to be
Constant
Yet warps with emotion
Slows with discomfort
Quickens with age
Disappears with sleep
Expands in dreams
Stops with death
The infinite remains

If luck is with Me
I will have
The time of my life

~ R. A. Whelan

Oh, how I do love thee!

As the snow still falls
and the ladder shakes
you call to me while
handing the snow rack

and comment:

Did you notice, your socks stink
and, I must remind you, your
dishes were left in the sink

As I scrape and pull from the top rung
at the four-foot drifts of snow and ice
I am thinking; if this ladder slips

Despite our years of love,
it won't turn out nice

Oh, how I do love thee
in this time of snow-emergency

How you hold firm the ladder
to prevent my fall and yet;
continue your chatter

How we are so alike and different too,
and now a stormy Valentine together
with which we can look back and say,

it's always been something new

- Thomas Wylie

February Fright

Lift the shovel and throw
no matter, this white stuff
has nowhere to go

At first it was a fun six inches
then plus four to make ten
but then doubled again

We begin to have a hunch
this winter could be sending
a very wicked punch

Kept inside as days pass by
told not to drive, stuck with worry
will we get out to resupply?

Days turn to weeks of white from the sky
in awe we watch; four feet, five feet,
six and more; now we can't open the door

Trapped; cord wood low and spirits too
emotionally we hang-on for March and
pray for a snow-free view

House now heavy with gigantic
mounds of snow and ice; and
within us concern grows, how
ends this February fright?

- Thomas Wylie

Holiday Survival

Mute the phone
garage the car
post a message
      no one home

Avoid the stores
throw out the mail
take long walks
      do the chores

Hide the credit cards
stop all news reports
order food online
      read the bards

Take this advice
and you'll be fine
with far less debt
      and a happy mind

~ Thomas Wylie

aliens

skin, blood, breath, eyes, teeth, and hair
we connect to each other by dreams,
hopes, fears; land sea and air

chains made, chains broken; they do
nothing but hold, torture, kill, push,
pull, imprison, or release the unspoken

parched earth, green grass, birds in flight,
clothes to carry, babies to hold; for thousands
of years millions and millions, by day and night

why, where, how; borders, fences, barriers,
mountains, rivers, snow, sun, sleet; what
ever where ever, we struggle on our feet

accepted, rejected, jailed or set aside, how
is that so many made it and thrive, yet turn
cold backs, toward thousands that die

you, me, we, they; all of us "others," on lands
that were not of our fathers and mothers

aliens

~ Thomas Wylie

Song of my PSA

PSA the PSA
who's to know
who's to say?

male body's tune that
will not go away

This is not your
Public Service Announcement
no, no, no
check the flow
Prostate Specific Antigen

Universally despised
male hate and dread
numbers to suggest alive
numbers to fear dead

Look and look again
PSA numbers are
not your friend

Drip, drip
samples into a cup

3.9, 4.3, 5.7
up, up, and up
trending or
mending?

Normal is a moving target

Flow easy flow out
flow stop
check the stream
long is good
short, and

Watch out!

Search sample and
Digital Rectal Exam
probing an unknown
that might be
inside the man

More men die with it than of it

Watchful waiting
active surveillance
trips and appointments
sleepless nights
quick stops
no lights

Biopsy
Gleason Scale
benign or inflamed
what does PSA data

say about your name?

- *Thomas Wylie*
twfrun@comcast.net

About the poet:
Thomas Wylie lives in Bradford, Massachusetts and currently teaches in the Graduate School of Education at Northeastern University. He's been writing poetry for 20 years; author of *Cold Car* (2014); and a member of the Haverhill River Bards. Tom's teaching career began on Panay Island, Philippines.

White

The benefits of skin color
appear at the oddest moments

when last in a check-out line of fifteen
all black but me; a white drug-store clerk
looks back and says

"May I help you?"

or, when seeking a city apartment and
the owner says if you help him find
other tenants you get a month rent-free,

looks you straight in the eye and whispers,

"But remember, we don't rent to blacks"

White:

unspoken privilege
you wear it always
never comes off

everyone sees it

- Thomas Wylie

Give it up

Give away all your money when you're not feeling prime
give your pain to the wind when it's not yet your time
give away your old clothes while they're still on your back
give that last can of beans take them all from the stack

Give away your old friends give away your old hat
give someone your husband your baby your flat
give it all up for nothing because that's where it's at
give it up pass it on then go out and come back

Give away your old worries they don't mean a thing
the more you give up the more you can sing
and when you are singing the more you can rise
and then you're not dying in anyone's eyes

The what you can make and the songs you can sing
dig them up pull them out   you won't hurt a thing
give it up   put it out you won't hurt a thing

~Toni Treadway

About the poet:
Toni Treadway runs the readings for the Powow River Poets at the Newburyport Public Library every other month. Her first poetry book *Late Harvest* came out in December 2018 from Kelsay Books.

A Good Holiday Season

It's a funny little world we live in. The news says that it's a good holiday season because sales are up 2.3 percent over last year. I hear that and just shake my head. I don't give a fig about companies getting rich and richer.

My holiday season has very little to do with money. (Like I have any anyway.)

It's a good holiday season for me when my four sisters and my brother and I are all under one roof laughing, playing cards and toasting the Mom and Dad, missing them and remembering Mom's crockpot cooking, and Dad reading *The Night Before Christmas* every December 24th.

It's a good holiday season when I get an unexpected phone call from my piano-playing pal who lives in Germany-and he plays me a tune over the phone! That's a wonderful holiday!

It'll be a good holiday season this Sunday when friends come over as I host a $1 Yankee Swap. It's a good holiday season when my days are filled with friends and beer and laughter and beautiful Christmas cards that fill my basket and fill my heart.

I hope you are having a good holiday season too.

~Tony Toledo

toledogoat@aol.com

About the storyteller:
Tony Toledo has been paying his rent by telling stories for the last 29 years. Peaches, beans and books show up, too. Tony believes stories and community are essential; he creates community with his tales and passes out coins infused with a year's good luck to poets, kids and folksingers, too.

Farewell Aunt Mary

My Aunt Mary Haley had pancreatic cancer. A friend was having a surprise 50th birthday party on Saturday, November 24th in Columbus, Ohio. I live in Beverly, Massachusetts (on the north shore of Boston). I went to Ohio because of my friend's birthday party. I went, we laughed, I yelled surprise and I sang happy birthday off key.

Since I was in Columbus I decided I was going to also visit Aunt Mary. On Sunday November 25th I drove the hour west from Columbus to Dayton to visit her. She was very jaundiced. She couldn't keep food down. She was still holding court wrapped in her electric blanket in the living room. She was still alert and laughing and talking. I got to hold her hand. I got to tell her I loved her one more time. I flew back to Boston Tuesday. Aunt Mary died Wednesday, November 28.

I flew back to Dayton the next Sunday to attend Aunt Mary's funeral on Monday, December 3rd. I arrived at St Luke's Catholic Church. Family and friends were gathering around Aunt Mary's casket to comfort each other with whispered stories of Aunt Mary. My cousin Dave turned to me and asked, "You're going to do Mom's eulogy right?" It was the first I had heard of it. Cousin Dave also said, "You're a professional storyteller. You got this in the bag." I was thinking this bag might have more than one hole in it.

There was a Drill Sargent of a woman from the church who power-walked up to me. "Are you cousin Tony? Come with me right now. Are you going to do the readings as well as the eulogy?" She showed me the readings, she showed me how I was to bow coming up to the altar, she told me to read loud and clear and not to rush. She told me she had copies of the readings for me to go over to be sure I could pronounce everything correctly. She said my five-minute eulogy was to focus on Aunt Mary's faith rather than her being funny. She said I was to sit on the end of the pew.

For the next twenty minutes I asked each of my five cousins to tell me one thing about their Mother and her faith and her life. I asked Uncle Jim the same. He said to be sure to say that he and Mary had been married for 70 years. I went to a side room and worked up an outline of different Aunt Mary stories that I had. I made sure to add the ones from her kids and husband.

During the funeral I was surprised I got a little choked up doing the readings more than the eulogy.

Mary Rose Haley was 91 years old. She was a nurse, wife, mother of 6, folk artist, sister and faithful Catholic. She loved Christ and knew her family loved her. I told about Aunt Mary hosting Thanksgiving with her six kids, the six from my family, and six more from more cousins, the Davises. She loved to host her extended family. She was faith in action. She also used a bingo blotter to paint her idea of a flower all over the kitchen walls and windows. She made sure her grandkids never took the Lord's name in vain. She always had a coffee for me. With her passing a door closed. Aunt Mary was the last of Mom's five siblings. My cousins and I have moved up a notch. We are now becoming the elders of the family. How did that happen?

My cousins told me I did good. I told them I could have done a lot better if they'd given me a little more time to pull the eulogy together. The death of their mother fogged their brains. I think each of them thought one of the others had asked me. Only as they were gathering before the funeral did they discover nobody had. I told them giving the eulogy was one last gift to Aunt Mary.

I long ago left the Catholic Church. I became a Unitarian. Later my cousin Dave said he had the fire extinguisher ready in case I burst into flames as I stepped to the altar. I read those Bible readings with respect and love. I read them loud so my almost deaf Uncle Jim could hear them. I read them so Aunt Mary could hear them. They were one last gift to the Aunt that I loved.

- Tony Toledo

At Country Club

1

The sunny summer day grows warm,
ladies and men begin to arrive for lunch
in the glassed-in porch laid out in linen,
a kind of aquarium overlooked by lawns
that slope greenly down. Ceiling fans
turn, oaring ripples of air across the room
in soft eddies. Guests in pairs murmur
to each other at the starched white tables,
where a crisp napkin stands waiting, and
the prongs and blades of all the forks
and knives gleam at each setting. We take
their orders for drinks, iced tea, coffee,
Arnold Palmers, cokes or Chardonnay.
The sinks at our stations brim with ice.
A Sicilian Apollo tends the bar. Steadily
they come, ladies, men. Order pads
tucked into our aprons, we flow to them
like cooling water over rock, pitchers
in hand. *What would you like? And how*
would you like that? Which do you prefer?
Gorgonzola or Swiss? Ciabatta or rye?
Russian or Caesar? Ice cubes clink
tumbling from the pitcher into glass.

2

It's Cerberus who guards the kitchens,
the steaming realms of griddle and stove
and red-hot toaster.
For you, no entrance.
Only chefs in their toques and white aprons,
and crewcut sous-chefs and the ancient
washer of dishes, his asbestos hands
slipping saucers and serving plates under
cascades of scalding water, may enter.
Your job to serve: Lift high the platters
of raw, sliced beef resting in its juice,
the gape-mouthed fishes with scales
that shimmer, the wild boar biting an
apple, or mandarin crab with his pincers.
Your job to bear them to those who wait,
demure, sipping their seltzer, their crisp
napkins folded into birds of paradise
spread out now, relaxing on their laps.
Only the chef with his smithy's fingers,
canny, beaked proboscis, and perfect recall
for sauces and sliced prosciutto
belongs to those realms of fire.
Listen,
if you like at the door, but do not enter--
you who were made only to bow and smile
and cajole with specials, noting precisely
the patrons' wandering desires on pads
that Hermes alone relays to those below.

3

Crazed in the flurry of summer,
I have to stand back for a second
or two, and let the customer wait,
wait to order, wait to eat, wait to wipe
their mouths when the plate's cleared.
For they thirst for water with ice,
for water without ice, for iced tea,
for drinks made just the way Apollo,
the downstairs barman, makes them,
with lots of ice and Absolut Vodka.
Or they've misplaced their napkin,
their fork, their daughter, their wife.
They would like to know, please, where
their mayo-on-the-side has gone, or
why their slice of toasted rye is
so long delayed. We all of us wait.
The waitstaff waits for the sous-chef
to give up some mayo, one waiter
waits for another to fold napkins,
polish knives, slice limes or lemons.
We wait for the drinks from Apollo,
whose real name is Bacchus.
We wait for our checks, for the sand
in the clocks to sink down into 3 o'clock
closing, for the last lonely patron,
a favorite of ours, to straggle out,
for the locks to click shut on the bar.

-Zara Raab
zara.raab@gmail.com

Zara Raab's books are *Swimming the Eel*; *Fracas & Asylum*; *The Book of Gretel*, and *Rumpelstiltskin.* Her work appears in *Verse Daily, River Styx, West Branch, Arts & Letters, Crab Orchard Review*, and *The Dark Horse.* She lives in Amesbury.

Where will Merrimac Mic go from here?

Mirroring
a tanka

I think of us all
reflecting inner beauty
some round-shaped some tall
no matter the mirror's shape
answering an inner call

Isabell
2019

Made in the USA
Middletown, DE
21 March 2019